FIREFIGHTERS
COLORING BOOK

NINA BARBARESI

DOVER PUBLICATIONS, INC.

Mineola, New York

The author wishes to thank
Lt. Daniel J. Williams
of the New York City Fire Department
for his assistance in preparing this book

NOTE

A firefighter's day begins at the firehouse, also known as an engine company. Fighting fires, rescuing people, and attending to injuries are all important parts of the job. Taking care of the equipment and making sure that it is ready when needed is also very important. Firefighters face great danger: flames, smoke, even a building collapse. The members of an engine company work together as a team—their lives depend upon it! Learn all about a day at an engine company as you color in the pictures in this book.

Bibliographical Note

Firefighters Coloring Book is a new work, first published by Dover Publications, Inc., in 2003.

International Standard Book Number

ISBN-13: 978-0-486-42646-4
ISBN-10: 0-486-42646-7

Manufactured in the United States by Courier Corporation
42646707   2015
www.doverpublications.com

Mike is a firefighter. He begins his day at Engine Company 39.

Mike walks in the front door of the station, passing the shiny red

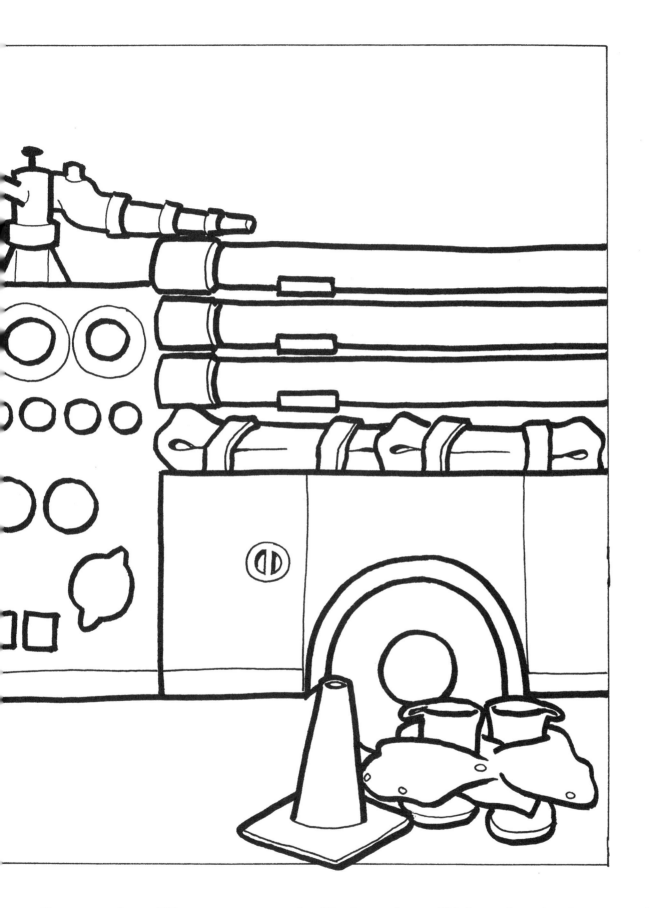

fire engine. The company's Dalmatian, Chips, is glad to see him!

Kevin and Patty are preparing a meal for the company in the firehouse kitchen. Mike says "Hi" to them on his way upstairs.

Mike is changing into his firefighter clothes, which he keeps in a locker.

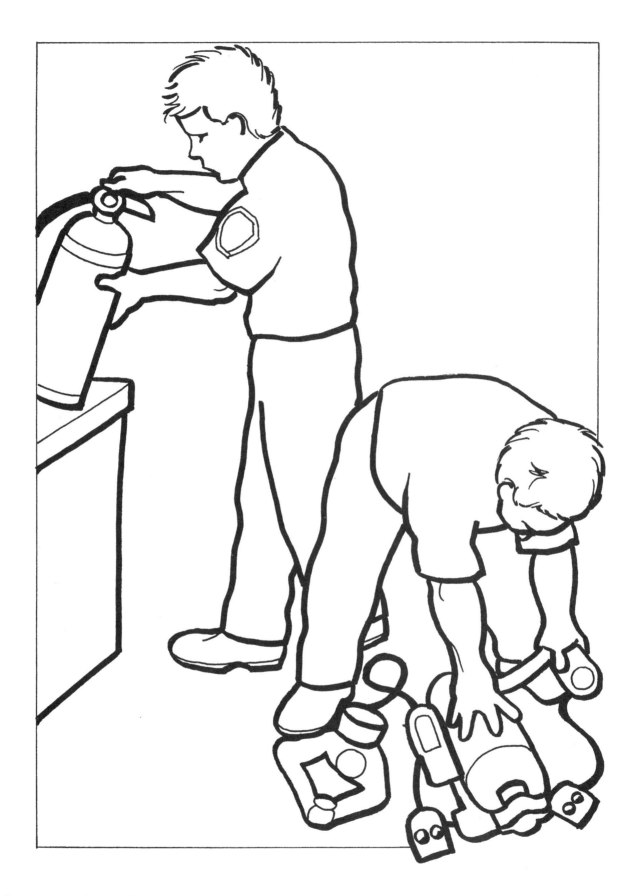

James is checking the pressure in the fire extinguisher.
Lou is making sure that the breathing equipment works.

6

Patty charges the batteries in the walkie-talkies, which the firefighters use to stay in touch. Kenny checks that the saw is ready.

Firefighters wear special clothing called "bunker gear."
This includes fire pants, coat, boots, and hard helmets

to protect their heads.

The fire engine gets very dirty when it is out on a call.

It's a big job for José and George to clean it!

Firefighters must always be prepared to use their skills, so they have frequent review drills. Lou and Mike are shown here forcing open a door.

Buildings must be inspected—checked for safety—regularly. Lieutenant Dan wants to have these boxes moved because they block an exit.

Firefighters are responsible for shopping for food, preparing meals for the company, and cleaning up the kitchen.

The firefighters share meals in the company's kitchen. In many ways, the members of an engine company are like a family.

In the middle of a calm, quiet afternoon, the fire alarm goes off!

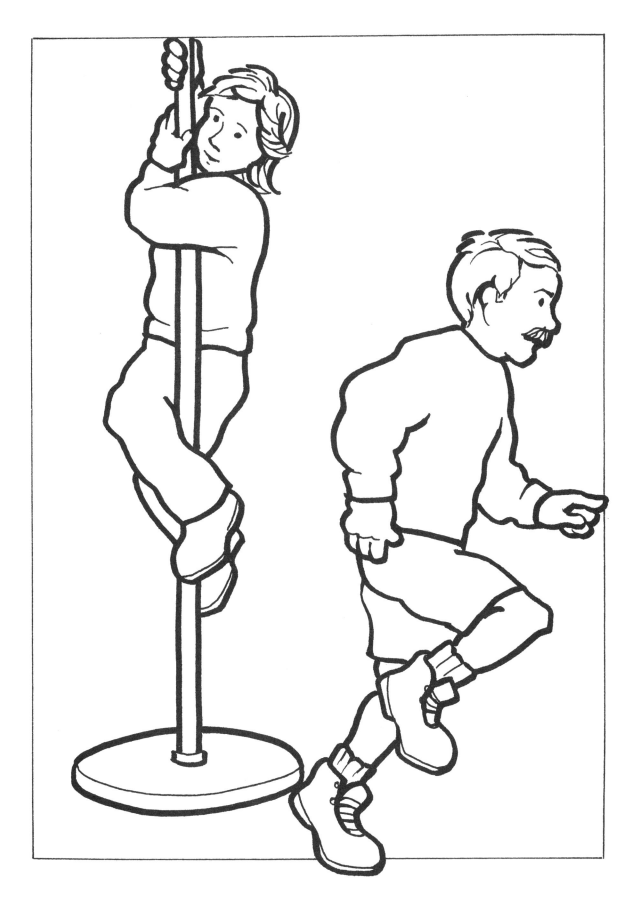

The firefighters are ready for action. They jump up from the table and move quickly to put on their bunker gear.

They buckle up their fire coats and climb into the waiting engine.

Mike runs outside to stop traffic so that the big engine can pull into the street safely.

Off they go! Chief Ed talks into the radio and the siren blares.

20

It's a big fire! Kevin jumps out of the driver's seat and opens
up the fire hydrant for water. Other firefighters pull the hose

out of the back of the engine. They grab tools and begin climbing up the ladders.

Whoosh! Water shoots out of the powerful nozzle of the
tower ladder. The firefighters are able to rescue everyone,

including this baby.

After making sure that the fire is out, the firefighters put the hose and tools back on the fire engines and trucks.

The firefighters drive back to the firehouse.

Kevin carefully backs the engine into the firehouse. Chips is happy to see his "family" again.

The entire company goes back into the kitchen, where they
will share a meal.

At the end of a busy day, Mike gives Chips his dinner.